TO THE DOGS

TO THE DOGS

POEMS

ROBERTA GOULD

Copyright @2016 Roberta Gould
All rights Reserved

Poems in this collection have appeared in Coffee House Press, Home Planet News, Waymark, Writing Air, Written Water, In Houses With Ladders, Not By blood Alone, Only Rock

With Special thanks to Malcolm McNeil
Artist, author, and a dog's best friend

By the Same Author:

Dream Yourself Flying
Writing Air, Written Water
Only Rock And Other Poems
Three Windows
Not By Blood Alone
Esta Naranja
Pacing The Wind
In Houses With Ladders
What History Trammels
Louder Than Seeds

Library of Congress Catalog Card number 20159221112
ISBN 978-0-6925-8875-8

Flame Tree Press

flametree@earthlink.net

http://robertagould.net

CONTENTS

Best Friend 1
On The Run 2
Found 4
They Never Reached You 5
Scanning 8
To Awake 10
Compensations 11
Day With Dog 13
Dog 15
Stray Dog 19
Off The Road 20
Community 22
Does A Dog Have Buddha Nature 23
Little Dog Run 25
Epiphany 27
I Decide To Wear My Eyeglasses 29
Delilah 31
Morning Walks 33
Her Cat I 36
Her Cat II 38
Little Things 40
Viet Nam 42
Taxco 44
Valiantly 46
Racoon 47
Elsa 49

Kitchen Moth   50
Off Day   52
Unearned Suffering   53
The World Does Not exist   55
Laggards   56
Dimanche   58
Epilogue for a Dog...(Lord Byron)   61
Sleeping Dog   64
Note 69

BEST FRIEND

She follows me around
and I give her the meat from my mouth to
keep her happy
She gives much relief
from freedom's space

so you could say she earns it
And there's more than enough for both of us It's
not a question of starving
Still, at times, I do it grudgingly confusing
myself with the truly hungry mired, as I
am, in a pond of delight with all
refinements
yet calling myself generous as
I hand her a tidbit— gone to
the dogs

ON THE RUN

Hi diddle diddle Where's
my dog gone four in the
morning still on the run?
The loud forest pulsates
Mice course the beams
scratch the old rafter
usurping my dreams
I shout and I holler there's
no dog in sight It's
almost an hour The sky's
growing light
but my dog doesn't come
I'm forced out of bed
get dressed in a jiffy
head for the road
with a leash that I jangle
and my whistle and call that
travel unheeded
till she trots down the hill
having chosen her moment
near the old sagging shack Hi
diddle diddle
my doggie is back

FOUND

Ant circles a dark world hemmed in
the lining of a jacket

The dog barks next door
hedged in by the yard

A shirt like a sail on a line
hangs hooked to trousers it can't move A

chair on the field tumbles over

Focus on any
without choice

Stay a while
It will give what it's got

THEY NEVER REACHED YOU

The pecans I packed with the apples
vanished between Delhi and Bright Hill
Perhaps they were left near the porch set
down when I let Duchess run

If they were devoured by bright black Clem and
Jim, the mangy retriever,
I'm glad—dogs need them more than we who
eat whenever we wish

And if I forgot them on the car roof as I
gathered my books, bags and acts a
swooping jay or fall squirrel
merits applause from these hands

Still, I eat one of the apples and fret
remembering the delight of pecans crowns
cracked open, in bags of ten
in Anahuac, and how these never reached you

But I'm glad, being the total picture,
until I remember the rain
earth's fungi, mold and bacteria
consuming precious pecan meat

My mercy is wanting I'm short
place my friends higher, more worthy than
little blue flowers nurtured,
and April's grass, with the loss

SCANNING

I've been searching the room for a
superfluous button puttering about
in the first person scanning the floor
though
the sweater can stay open
I'm just setting the morning in motion

Then a porcelain plate slides off the desk and
the dog explores her palate
carefully probing a yam with her tongue gobbling it
down
The two white halves are tossed in the trash and I
continue my search
though I note an extra button
the kind knitter imagining this future
sewed on to replace what falls off

Yet the quest goes on! And
more time is spent
It's a puzzle-solving mystery
what defines us
not how chromosomes are suppressed
molecules encircling them to deactivate
but this simple persistent scanning of a floor as the
sun shines in

TO AWAKE

Again the knotted fur
tugged hard with teeth is
groomed Clock turns The
sun rises again

If the dog keeps on and
the little beetles
do their yearly invasion flying
drop from the ceiling

can't the one sleeping
under them do the same
open eyes   stir   move
drink a glass of water?

COMPENSATIONS

He takes the elegant black woman's arm and his
guide dog
is superfluous
With uncertain balance he
walks towards the bus
sunglasses askew, tilting left

New to darkness
that thick-featured hulk of a man
hands of a laborer
and nose that is pure scar tissue is
blissed by her sweet attention and
grins broadly
walking slower than before There

are some compensations

DAY WITH DOG

Six chickens tripped down the road ignoring a
cat that passed
and the woman's horse

A couple of goldfinch
approached the house
first time in a decade

and vanished into an apple tree These
and a few unknown sounds... a new
species? birds in distress?

and crickets starting to click
along with the katydids filled
the air like a city

all afternoon as you and I
watched each other
through the screen separation

you guarding me from the living
outside the shed with its cedar fragrance where I
sat, forever, and said nothing, like you

DOG

1.
She swells with fury
charges the door snarling
her anus dilating

2.
Cocks her head
hears wall sprits...whines an hour drops
down exhausted

3.
On her side heaving
in sleep..legs straight out...the air near
her body hot

4.
Teasing the cat in the morning
her growl is feigned
all teeth and delight

5.
One grand barking bout
all night...a drunk comes into the
hall...it's nothing

6.
Then out for her walk the
house grows still
you can hear your heart beating

7.
The sheets marked where
she nuzzled your limp hand and
woke you up laughing

8.
Friday's event..a black
dusty bone in the hall where she
carried it stealthily

9.
The cat ventures out
to the rainy ledge does not bother
to look back

10.
Home from her walk in ten minutes
(ten years.) she races in
mad with joy

11.

Hassles the cat..shaking a shoe
jumping up to lick you
her thick paw raking your leg

12.
"Get off!" you command, she
circles the linoleum
noisy nails scraping and sliding

13.
When you kiss me she
whimpers..I reach out and pet
her You don't like it

14
But she does
and flops to the floor exhausted
beside the bed falls asleep

STRAY DOG

Will staring at the sun
cook him down to blank slumber
free of his ragged ears' pain
and the red speckled flesh
that shocks the vacationer's eye?

In the thin shade of the beached
boat's hull, will he cool off better
to bear the red mange that hunger
has given him
bones visible through bald flesh?

When I feed him he can't hold it down I'm
traveling, can't take him in
can't nurse him to health
So I imagine a shot in the skull as
he finally eats a dreamed meal but I
know this is a lazy way
and precludes a miracle

Doing or not doing won't help

OFF THE ROAD

I could not tell how weary I was
until three dogs at dusk
trotted up in the mist to be petted

We walked off the road to a frozen pond Teasing
they chased each other and slid Then the big
curly one

pressed her head against me I
spoke She wanted affection It
was easy to give

All the eyes in the city of millions had
set off a great need to love
And I was tired of that old condition

COMMUNITY

When a furry friend bites seed pods from paws
breathes hard and rests from rounding the pond I
watch from a chair

If I start to founder
she'll stroke her way out,
snatch my hair and tug me to shore

If she whines for her meal
when the snows cover everything I'll
dish it out like a mother

It's good too live in community

"DOES A DOG HAVE BUDDHA NATURE?"
The Master Asked

I live in a hole
It's cozy down here
Self-sufficient I eat
dirt and pebbles
I process minerals
develop a gizzard
and robots do my work As I
observe the weather safe in
my enclosure
I become a philosopher
Though the food is sparse I
happily reduce
body and mind
then give up language

Fowl?
Mole?
Buddha?

Me?

LITTLE DOG RUN

I didn't let the little dog rest Restless I
got up four times an hour to look for
her candy medicine
or to putter in the kitchen

As dawn approached
I poured myself a shot It
had small effect
though weariness wasn't lacking

So I turned on the radio
and kept going
till the new day began
I stopped, then, took up

where I'd left off
the day before
free of words, finally, the
body's needs muted

and watched the little dog
asleep, despite me,
quiver and start to run in
the air, in her dream

EPIPHANY

Forgive me my
dog
I was bad I
thought
myself blind to you
on the cushion your
mistress never
petting you I
was busy with politics
never caressing your royal head To
you
I bow
to be at your level
beg forgiveness
you who merit more
than I do
you who harm no one simple
in your appetites patient in
your infinite love to you I
humbly dedicate this
epiphany

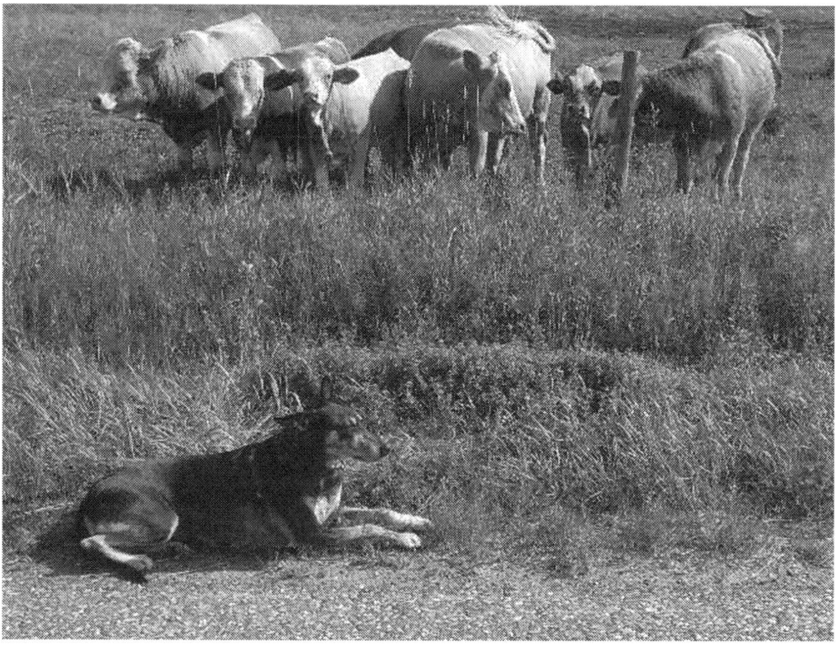

I DECIDE TO WEAR MY EYEGLASSES

I denied myself clear sight, hairs
near a nostril grown, front
speckle of her snout. like her
belly, pink and brown

I took to wearing glasses to
perceive her better then
each whisker's differing length
to the side or under under her chin

The curls that topped her head like
a dancer's uncombed coif charmed
me out of my wits
I refused to take them off

The cabbage leaf I ate
was a land with roads and hills
Rivers like arteries flowed revealed
topography's cells

My own hands, too, were a tale
more real than any book
nails and skin vision
anywhere I'd look

POMPEII DOG

DELILAH

When the sun takes your tracks
with their mountain of snow and
lifts them to heaven vaporized,
invisible,
I'll pass the trailer they buried you beside absorb
the grass you nourish

If I continue to love my drunken neighbors I'll
keep growing as your wiry hair continues to
grows in the earth
But your happy jaw loose with light panting after
the wonder of running the forest
and your deep sleep on the oak floor

is what I'd rather repeat in
the joy of freedom
that continues, tempered without you dreaming up
magical moments
those routine days that always amused and
challenged me
with your persistent nudging and love

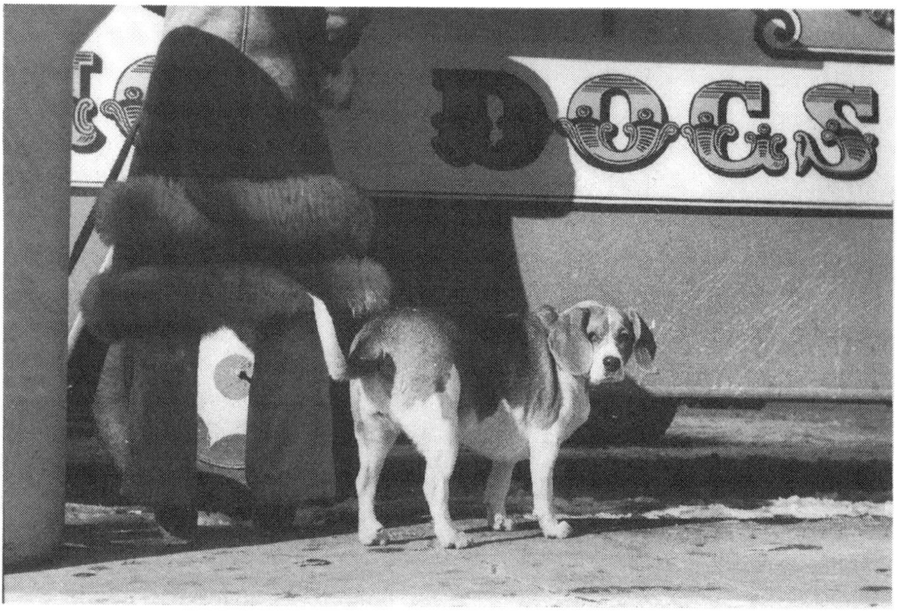
DOGS

MORNING WALKS

I.
Nobody walks the path but the two of us years
now and still the trees watch
The beings who inhabit the leaves
or burrow into the bark with powerful pincers are
invisible to us who've seen them in pictures or
crunched and eaten a few
who've strayed near the house

There is no tale to tell no
encounter or drama
New shoots sprout like dense cathedrals beside
the pond where the path ends
and a mottled sky mantles mottled pavement as
cogitation gives way
to the ground under our feet

II.
The solid road is glazed and we walk cautiously
Branches as sentinels bowed with the freezing poise
transparent arrows

Nothing to fear, canine, feline and I Perfect
flowers of ice
and glass shoots promising buds
mark our passage

Networks of twigs, dendrite and synapse are
the sky's crystals
till one and another crack
leaving arcs of shards and broken wood Where
will this be in an hour?

And when the rain drips from melting roofs who
will swim?

HER CAT

She is at the screen looking in I
know she wants to join us
but I do not get up and open the door tired
after our afternoon walk

"Who am I?" one of us asks "In
or out?" whoever is seeing
I call to her but she no longer comes
I lean back and write but she is dreaming

or forgets--I don't know
ignorant of where I myself have landed and
what wings I wore when I flew
and where I came from where I am now

though I hear a distant dog bark a
sharp chorus of crickets
and the cool air that enters changing me this
night that begins to start

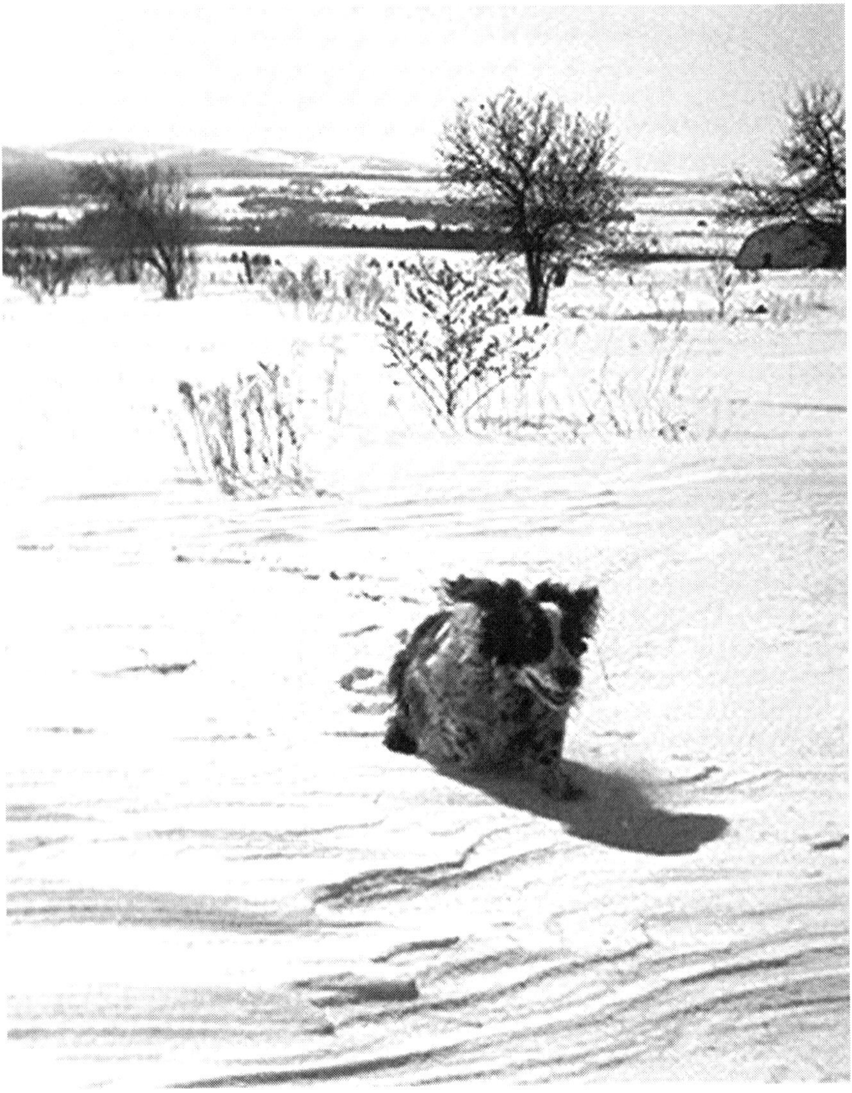

HER CAT

Alice was gone
curled on the wicker chair the
one with the green pad under
the kitchen table

She vanished fast
and the room turned empty
Only the utensils and furniture remained and
lovely light that now was irrelevant

There was no more meowing
Her dog came to sniff
cold snout confirming I was there
Then she dropped to the floor and slept

I was lost. Didn't know what to do, all
the books read, people gone,
and I wasn't hungry The
world small as a jail

I wanted to scream
But I was too old for that And
the voice of the wind
was enough to assure my silence

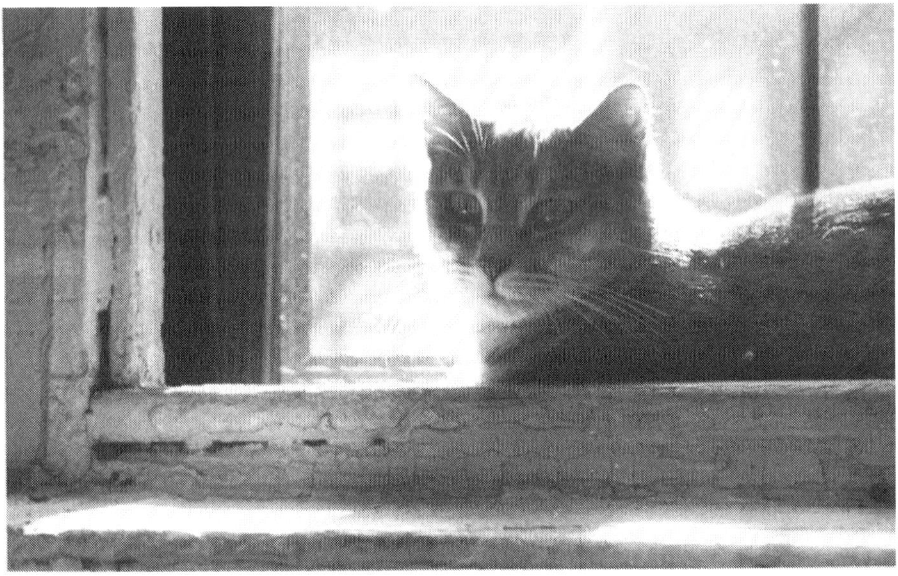

LITTLE THINGS

A bank like a pig a
rake like a fork
and hands you'd find on a frog
with a bit of imagination

On a match box
there's a painting of creation
flowers sprouting in April and a
rutted driveway
beside a lost glove

In the city a shower
is a curved faucet leaking
a cat stretching to drink and stay dry and
the buzz of traffic below
which is no Christmas train set

No grand scheme takes you in No
fretting or strutting
Just little things And
you're happy!

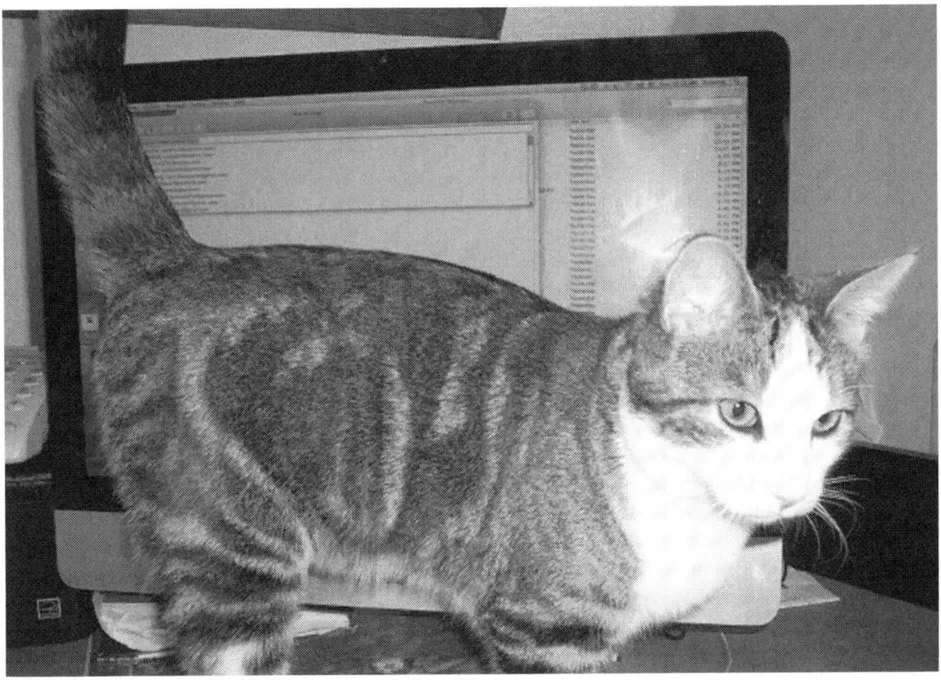

VIET NAM

Beds flung over tree
A dog stalking the wreckage a
genocidal pilot
trailing while clouds of silk
through the red night sky till
he's captured
in the center of Hanoi

Why they do not tear him apart is
an imponderable
of the human heart

BEWARE OF DOG

TAXCO 2001

What are they doing all day in
that grand mystery called
"work?"

I wander around
till the sun goes down
from here to there and back again while
she twists string
and he falls from a scaffold
breaks a few bones in his back

I hold fruit in my hands
And in yours there's a gadget to fix time,
bring back the past
tomorrow,
hold what we may not
have seen.

Suddenly a dog yelps
and cars keep passing
like ants on a mission
round the plaza

The whole town works
even the crumpled up creature
in a special chair outside the church named
for an ancient martyr

After this we return to our room
and sleep
dream it transformed to
our special vision It is
night
The dogs yelp again We
awake
lie still and listen

VALIANTLY

As she circles the kitchen island I
remember Therese
rounding her bed
on her last pilgrimage,
eyes glazed with glory, the bliss of rising
higher than the Rome she wouldn't reach as
she uttered something inaudible
in her final days before someone who knew,
or didn't know, gave her the name "Little Flower"

Duchess the Spaniel is eating her kibble outside
in the cold she was born to, relishing the brisk
new air
gazing to earth or to sky
Everyday as she loops round the isle
sniffing for crumbs or invisible life
on the tile floor, I imagine she is remembering
everything, as the saint did,
in a grand synthesis of life, this
canine mother

Unable to travel far, to Bethlehem, in illness, or the
tree a mile away, in her nineteenth year, they affirm
life's existence
valiantly

RACOON
   for Gioia Timpanelli

The black tip of its pointed snout was still shining though a
few flies buzzed about
It smelled a bit
but was not yet carrion

It's gone today
Only a bone and teeth are strewn in
the grass that is turning to hay
and I remember the scratch at the door how
it nosed its way in
spent the winter asleep on the coverlet of
the one who lived here before me and fed
its clan thirteen summers

When these teeth are sown
and the dogs stop
reeking of death
will I, perhaps, forget it
when the field is clear of any remnant and
I pass each morning, newly risen?

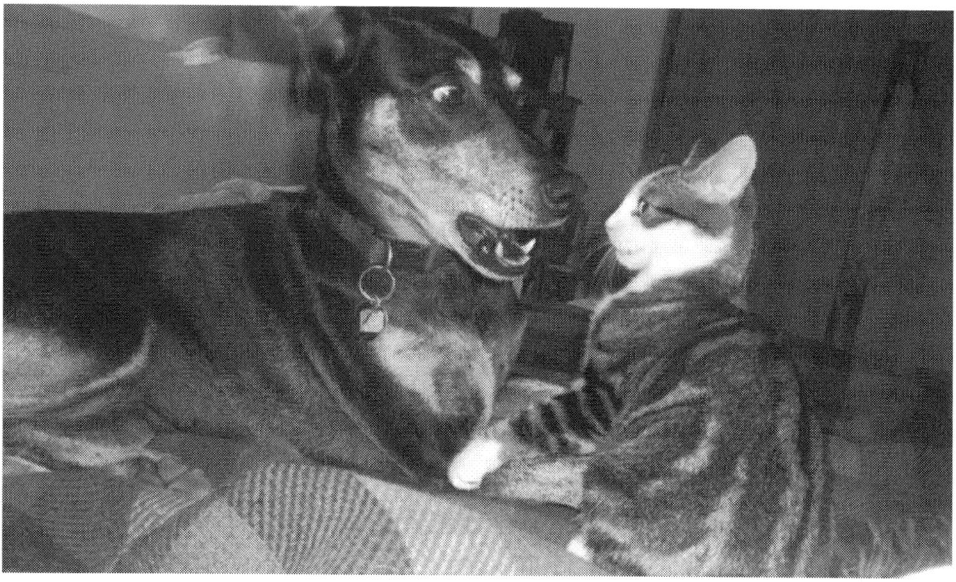

ELSA

It's no chore pitching in feeding
the sheep
taking her dog to the vet
or hearing her chatter as she rummages for
rope or a knife
It's a pleasure being there cooking
for her or wheeling hay
to where they ruminate behind glazed eyes

Today she captured a lamb, pure white, who
had taken a notion to separate
and run across the lawn near the highway She
carried her airy and mild
to the proper side of the fence
then shook the hose and turned it on so
the flock might drink

KITCHEN MOTH

Chicken broth drips from the ladle as
you flavor the puppy's kibble
A heavy moth beside the bowl,
black spots on yellow, perches dead still Have
you scalded it, you ask yourself?
Is it another kitchen death
like the spider washed down the drain or
the June bug battered after the rain? No.
When you sweep it into your palm cover it
with the other one
it spreads its wings, reveals a pink center
flutters, flies off and is gone

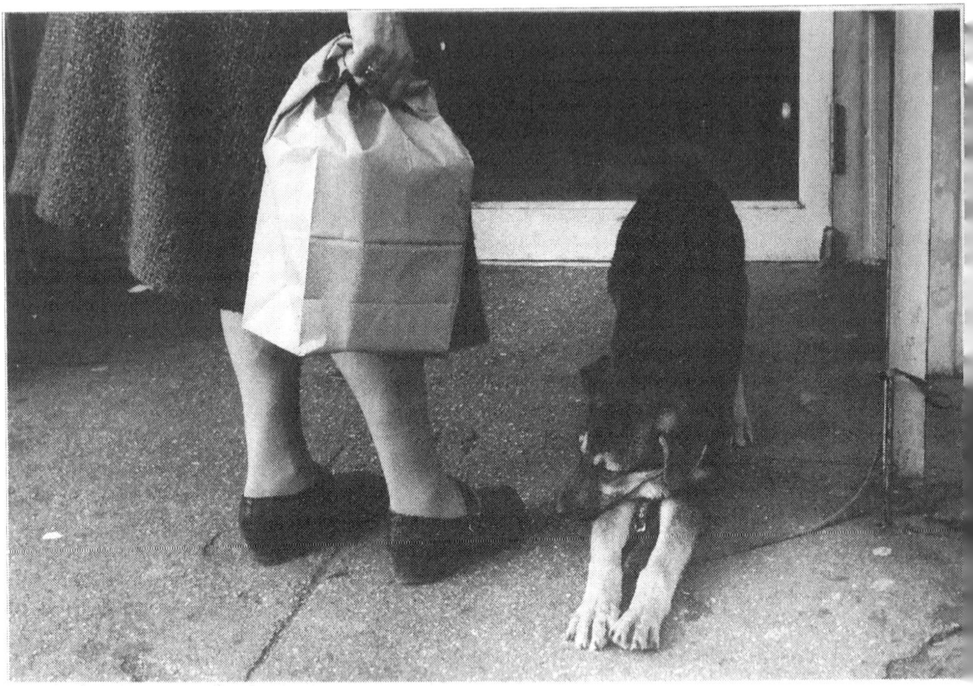

OFF DAY

Everything slips
The pot handle burns

Eggs splatter the floor
The matches spill

Books fall off the shelf
Can't find the stamps

The pen dries up powder
dots the rug

The teapot cracks The
dog is lost

UNEARNED SUFFERING
for Kirby Congdon

Don't blame me
if I have not earned
my suffering
I who have everything
shoes, roof, a borrowed dog
and the ground unexploded,
under me.
Don't judge too harshly if
I cry
and have not labored for my tears If
you don't believe me
go to the movies
but hold back your brilliance
Don't attack
I'm truly sorry I fail
and am not the voice of the century as
you promise to be
It's that I saw my dreams
and refused to be silent So
say nothing
if you can't credit me
for I have consoled myself
with this poem I send you I
who am your thief of woe

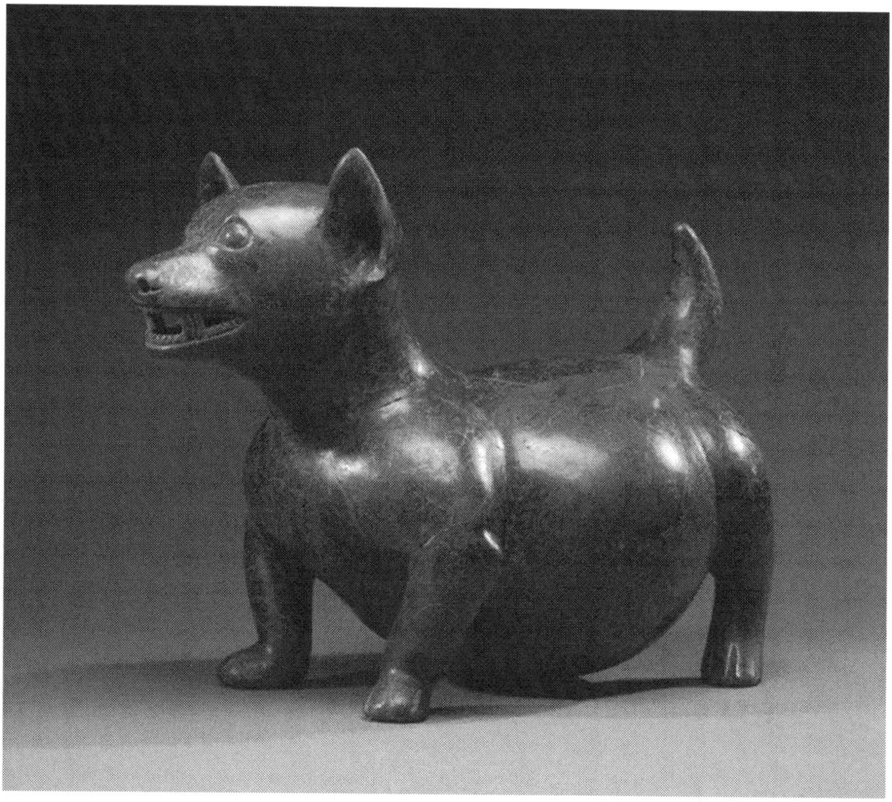

THE WORLD DOES NOT EXIST

The little pasha in his carriage intent
on the orange framed mirror in his
hands
as his father pushes him
through Central Park tree
buds open
and toy dogs scurry to keep up with
their long-legged mistresses also out
for an hour, leashed

The child fixes on his reflection as
yellow blossoms begin
His father can't see his face holds
admiration in abeyance and
wheels him
A god in his carriage!
alone

LAGGARDS

What matter they're last,
linger in the grass,
rise and circle back to
the stand of trees over
the pond,
dotting the bare branches
crackling the sky with their prattle?

The wind stirs, the clouds move a
dog watches
Not simply the scouts
but the whole flock has flown off The
laggards do not worry cavorting,
chattering
at pond's edge

as a few leaves spin down,
the sun comes out
and the dog drinks
Finally, they take off,
black wings into the invisible

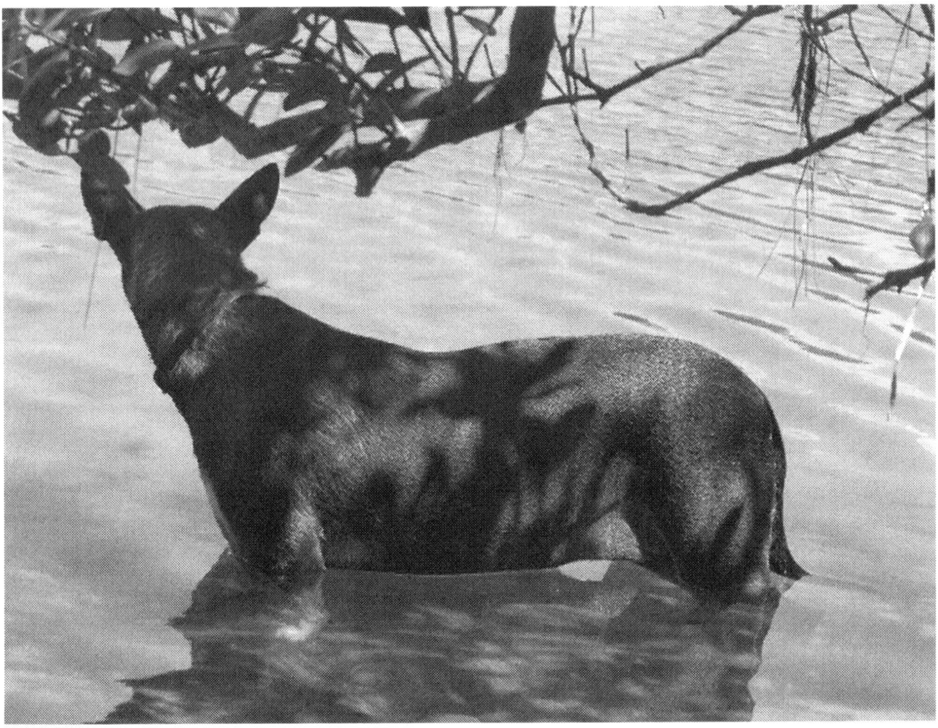

DIMANCHE

I'm losing my voice
I can't find my speech
Where is my face
the one I believed
or imagined?

Dogville was where
my language was broadcast
tones for the moment
commands or cooing
as required

But years have passed
I'm breathing, yes,
though I can't talk with
my fellows
I have forgotten how or
never knew how can
only say
"The coffee is good"
or "What a waste this war is—
the accumulation of human treasure"

Most agree
There's nothing new in these assertions but
such talk bores many
who seek thrills
and the speed of stimulation

As the dog licks her paws
and the cat sleeps on her chair I
close the book of my day tongue
tied
and happy

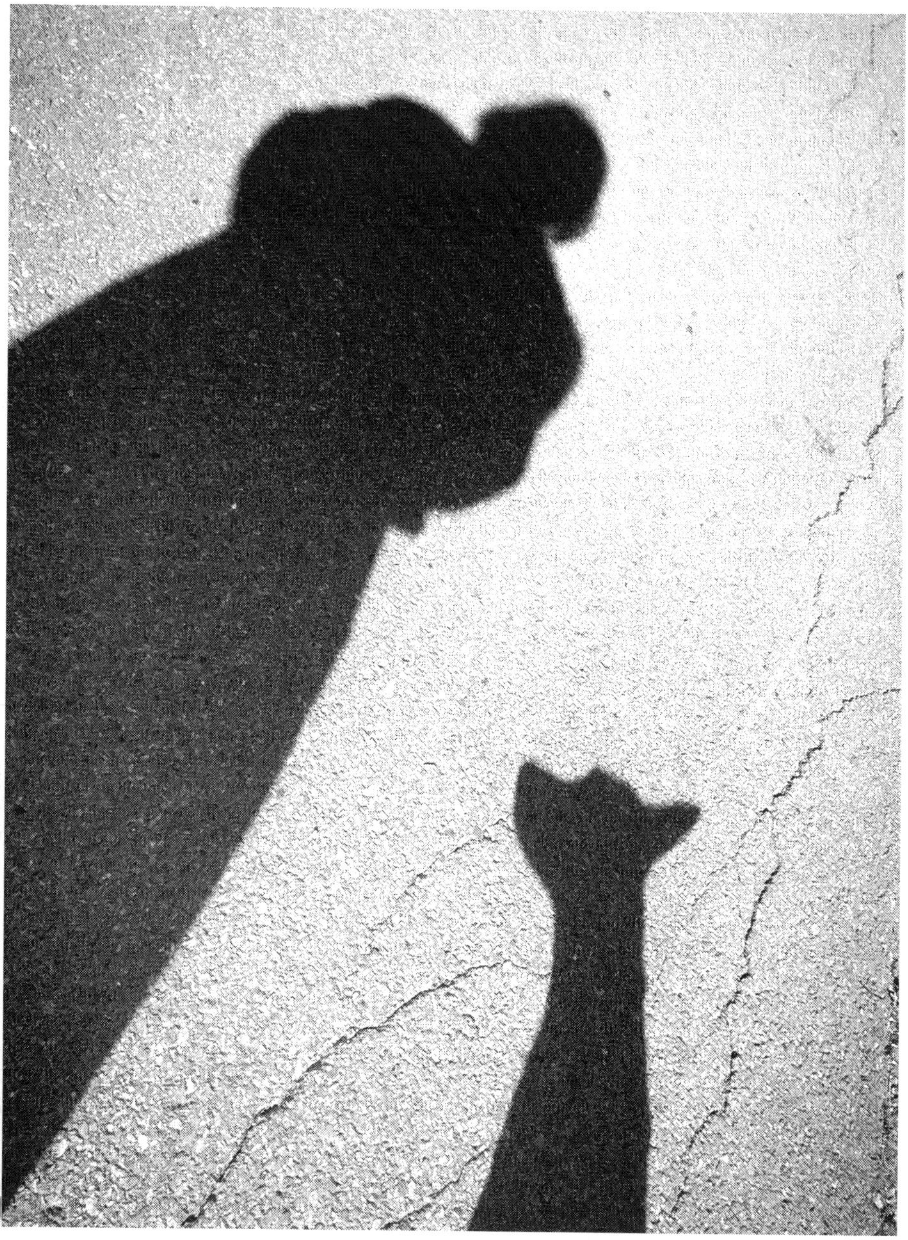

EPITAPH TO A DOG
…Lord Byron

When some proud Son of Man returns to Earth, Unknown to Glory, but upheld by Birth,
The sculptor's art exhausts the pomp of woe, And storied urns record who rests below.
When all is done, upon the Tomb is seen,
Not what he was, but what he should have been. But the poor Dog, in life the firmest friend,
The first to welcome, foremost to defend, Whose honest heart is still his Master's own,
Who labours, fights, lives, breathes for him alone, Unhonoured falls, unnoticed all his worth, Denied in heaven the Soul he held on earth – While man, vain insect! hopes to be forgiven, And claims himself a sole exclusive heaven.

Oh man! thou feeble tenant of an hour, Debased by slavery, or corrupt by power – Who knows thee well, must quit thee with disgust,
Degraded mass of animated dust!
Thy love is lust, thy friendship all a cheat,

Thy tongue hypocrisy, thy heart deceit! By
nature vile, ennobled but by name,
Each kindred brute might bid thee blush for
shame.

Ye, who behold perchance this simple urn, Pass
on it honor none you wish to mourn. To mark a
friend's remains these stones arise; I never knew
but one -- and here he lies.

           ...... Lord George Gordon Byron

Epitaph To A Dog

'Inscription on the Monument to a Newfoundland Dog' was
written in honor of Lord Byron's Newfoundland dog,
Boatswain, who had just died of rabies. When Boatswain contracted the
disease, Byron reportedly nursed him without any fear of becoming
bitten and infected. The poem is inscribed on Boatswain' tomb which is
larger than Byron's, at Newstead Abbey, Byron's estate.

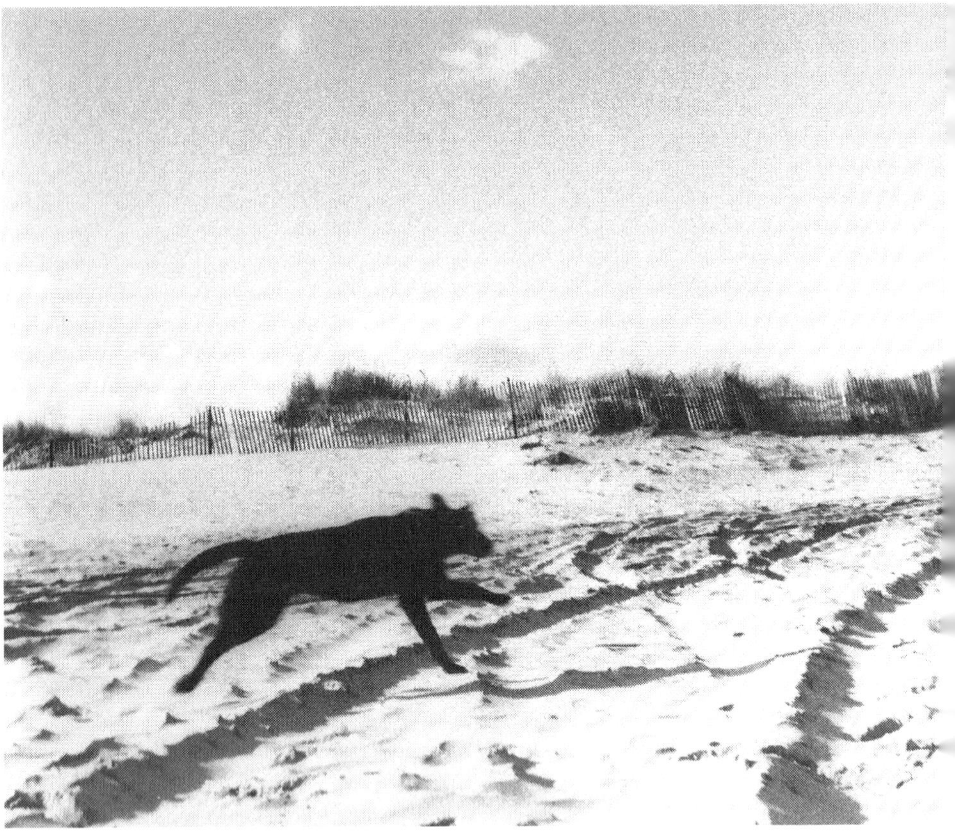

SLEEPING DOG

I didn't move her from the bed though
it was the shedding season her hairs,
short and many revealed by the
morning light
as she shook herself awake

So that's why I wheeze!
I resolve
to confine her to the cushion but I
forget
leave the door open
descend to do important things
read while I wash the coverlet
covered with her short hairs

When I return I find her where I left her and I
tell her to leave
She is sleeping   I don't insist
and run the hand held vacuum over her

She opens an eye, docile as usual,
doesn't move
Someone else might be killing her!

Freedom is difficult
She sleeps

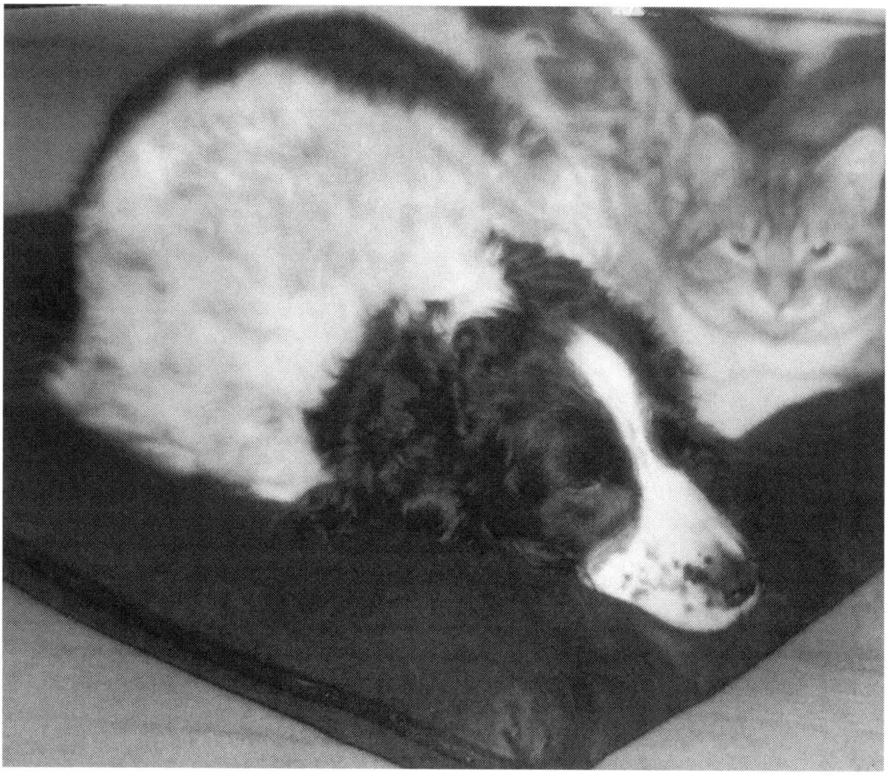

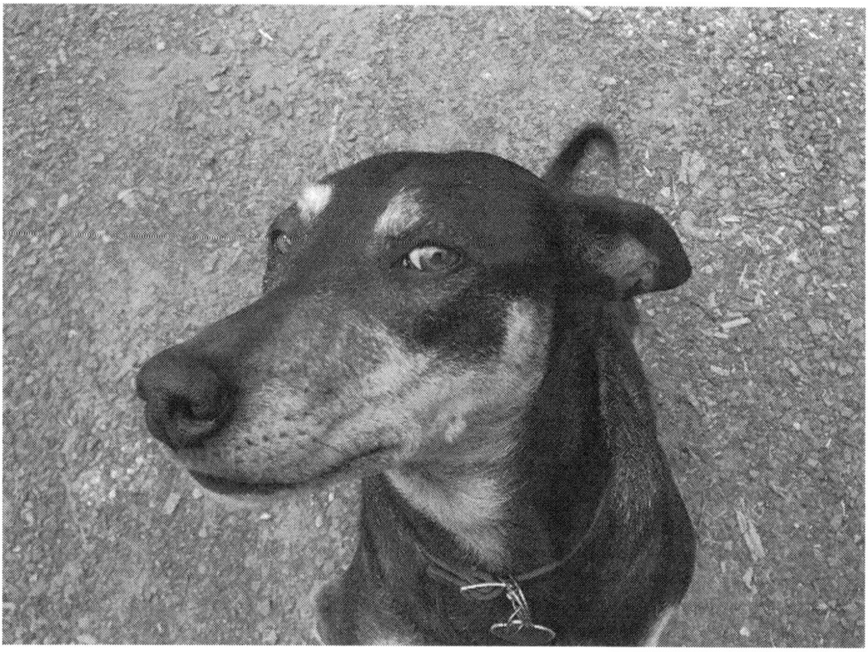

A Note About the Author

Roberta Gould's 10th book of poems, Louder Than Seeds, Foothills Publishing, was preceded by Pacing the Wind, Shivistan Press and In Houses With Ladders, Waterside Press. Her themes are varied with powerful political poems often ironic, never pedestrian. In Mexico, where she studied Filosofía y Letras at the UNAM, she organized a responsible tourism campaign after teaching Spanish at Brooklyn College and the University of California in Berkeley. Several hundred of her poems have appeared in poetry reviews. Anthologies include *The* Art and Craft of Poetry, editor Daisy Aldan; *Mixed Voices*, Milkweed Editions: *Rage Before Pardon*; *A Slant of Light,* Cod Hill Press Books; *Up the River.*
She has translated poetry from the Spanish and Catalán.
Other photographs and poems can be found on her web site: robertagould.net and at Twitter. She resides in the Hudson Valley with her dog, Lily, who was a stray from a beach near Santo Domingo, and who is trilingual.